Matchstick Mini and grief

By Edel Malone

Original concept created, illustrated, and written by Edel Malone. I'm sure you will love these books as much as I do. I know you will enjoy making lasting memories with your child moving forward in all stages of their lives by encouraging your child to tell you what's on their mind throughout their lifetime. Asking questions is the way forward. Check out some of the other Matchstick Mini books. Sizes and colors may vary for printed books.

The Matchstick Mini books are designed to encourage your child to open up and talk about what is on their mind from an early age. The topics covered are related to young children to encourage good communication techniques carrying on into each stage of their lives, keeping safety and values in mind.

OTHER BOOKS FROM MATCHSTICK MINI

Matchstick Mini and safety

Matchstick Mini and others

Matchstick Mini has fun

Matchstick Mini and school

Matchstick Mini is very good

Matchstick Mini is healthy

When an adult explains to Matchstick Mini that Fluffy is gone to heaven and he won't be coming back, Matchstick Mini can't understand where Fluffy, other people, or animals go when they die. Matchstick Mini doesn't understand what that means. All the adults tell Matchstick Mini his cat fluffy, and all the other people and animals that died are okay, and they are happy and at peace in heaven.

Matchstick Mini still doesn't understand what heaven is or why or where people or animals go when they die. He chooses to believe that they are happy and healthy in heaven. Do you know any people or pets that have died and gone to heaven?

Matchstick Mini knows it is okay to feel sad because Fluffy died, and he hugs his family when he feels sad. Matchstick Mini loved Fluffy so much that the thought of not seeing him again makes him feel sad. Matchstick Mini knows it is normal to feel sad, and he knows it is okay to feel happy too. Fluffy would want Matchstick Mini to enjoy his life and be happy. Do you know that it is okay to feel sad and it is okay to feel happy too?

Matchstick Mini knows it's okay to miss Fluffy, and he misses all the fun times they had together. Matchstick Mini knows it is good to talk about Fluffy and how sad he feels. Fluffy would want Matchstick Mini to be happy and have fun remembering all their happy memories and enjoy his life.

Matchstick Mini knows it is okay to talk to people or pets that have died in his head because it helps him feel happy, and he likes to tell them that he misses them, and he likes to tell them his good news too. Matchstick Mini knows it is normal to talk to Fluffy even though he is not around anymore, and he feels close to Fluffy and Matchstick Mini believes Fluffy can hear him.

Matchstick Mini likes to think about Fluffy and all the happy memories he had with his cat. Thinking about Fluffy makes Matchstick Mini smile. Matchstick Mini loves remembering all the fun he had with Fluffy and the games they used to play too. Do you have happy memories to remember about your pets or people that have died?

At night time, Matchstick Mini likes to say goodnight to his cat Fluffy in his head because he knows Fluffy can hear him from heaven. Matchstick Mini likes to talk to Fluffy in his head at night time and he tells Fluffy he is going to have a great sleep and wake up early to enjoy the next day. Matchstick Mini knows when he sees butterflies, robin redbreasts, and feathers; these are signs that Fluffy says hello.

Matchstick Mini knows that some people don't have funerals and not everyone gets to go to every funeral for pets or people that died, and that's okay. Everyone can do different things. Matchstick Mini and his family have a little get-together in the garden to say goodbye to Fluffy. Matchstick Mini likes to talk to his family about Fluffy, and he loves to talk to them about whatever is on his mind.

Matchstick Mini knows that not everyone gets buried in a special graveyard when they die, and that's okay. Some people get cremated and have different ways to pay respect when someone dies. Matchstick Mini and his family dig a grave to bury Fluffy in the back garden. Sometimes Matchstick Mini likes to sit beside Fluffy's grave and talk to Fluffy and tell Fluffy what is on his mind.

Matchstick Mini knows not all pets or people that have died have a grave to visit. Some people have a cremation, and there is not always a grave. Anyone can choose to remember people or pets whenever they want to. Matchstick Mini's friend has a vase called an urn on the mantlepiece to remember his family member that died. Matchstick Mini's friend likes to talk to the urn when he feels happy and sad. Matchstick Mini and his friend won't touch the urn because it is very special, and no one wants it to get broken. They know the urn is special and not a toy to play with.

Matchstick Mini knows it's okay if adults are upset and feel sad about Fluffy or other people and pets that died because they knew Fluffy, and they loved him too. Matchstick Mini knows his family has lost other people they loved, and he likes to ask questions about them and talk about everyone who has died and gone to heaven to keep their memory alive.

Matchstick Mini loves talking to his family about Fluffy, his cat, and he loves talking to his family about all the happy memories he had with Fluffy. Matchstick Mini understands that everyone can remember people or pets who died whenever they want, and they can choose nice memories to remember about all the fun times they had together. Matchstick Mini misses Fluffy, and he knows Fluffy will miss him too. Matchstick Mini will never forget Fluffy because of all the lovely memories and happy time they spent together.

Matchstick Mini tells his friends when he is sad, and his friends get him to have fun by playing games and chatting about their day and any good news they have. Matchstick Mini is always happy about other people's good news. Matchstick Mini knows that anyone who died would like him to be happy and have fun. Matchstick Mini knows he should never feel guilty about having fun because Fluffy would want him to be happy.

Matchstick Mini starts to accept that Fluffy is gone, and he accepts Fluffy is in a happy place. Matchstick Mini believes Fluffy is looking down on him, and he believes Fluffy wants him to enjoy his life and be happy and have fun. Fluffy loved all the fun times he had with Matchstick Mini, and Matchstick Mini is grateful for all the time he spent with him and grateful to have had Fluffy in his life.

Printed in Great Britain
by Amazon

32455890R00021